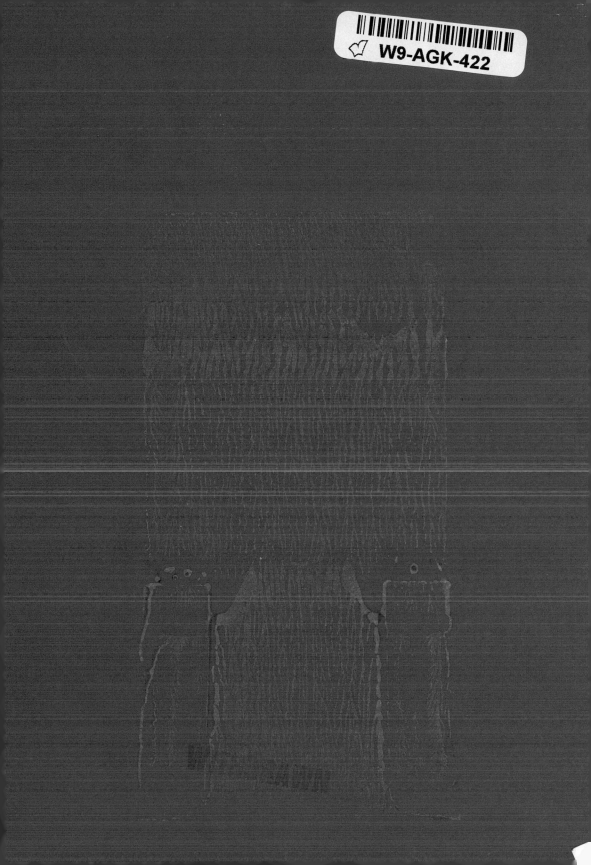

WORDS
inside
WORDS

by

Michael Aage

Illustrated by Arnold Spilka

Philadelphia • **J. B. LIPPINCOTT COMPANY** • *New York*

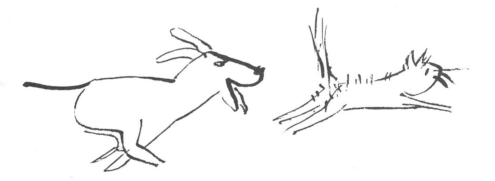

DID YOU KNOW
you can find
WORDS INSIDE WORDS????

For example...
Inside of DOG
you can find DO.
Inside of CAT
you can find AT.

THERE ARE MANY WORDS HIDDEN INSIDE
OTHER WORDS.

LET'S SEE WHICH ONES WE CAN FIND...

If you look hard you'll see
there's an OX inside of BOX
and a RAT inside of CRATE.

You might not be surprised
to find a COT inside of COTTAGE
or US in HOUSE.

But imagine finding TEN in TENT!

Here are some surprises.
If you look in BOWL
you can find OWL
and in SINK
there's INK.
Look in the BATHTUB
and you'll find BAT.
In CUPBOARD it may really surprise
you to find BOAR
and in CORNER you have CORN.

Sometimes letters of a hidden word
are not next to each other
and have to be moved around.
For example:

In PACKAGE
you can find CAGE.

If you look in PRESENT
you will find PEN

and TABLE has TALE.

In these next words you will have to move
the letters around a little more
if you want to find BEAR
inside of BARREL
and CUB in BUCKET

or to find SKATE
inside of BASKET
and CAT in ATTIC.

Some words become other words by moving ALL
the letters around to form the new words.

SO

In ART
you can find TAR
and in WORDS
there is SWORD.
It's nice to know
in ODOR you can find DOOR
and in SWING you find WINGS

But did you know

there's a SHRUB in BRUSH

or a LUMP in PLUM

or HOSE in SHOE?

We saved a surprise for the last.

In ARMY you can find MARY!

There are words to find wherever you are.
Here are some you can find
if you are outside.

Of course there's TREE
in STREET

and CUR
in CURB

and RAIL
in LIBRARY

and TUG
in GUTTER

But imagine finding GOWN
in WAGON

BOAT
in AUTOMOBILE

DART
in HYDRANT

LAMB
in MAILBOX

and SEAL
in BASEBALL!

If you're at home, here are some things
you might find:

A WIND in WINDOW.
And while you're there you might find
a PIN in RAINDROP
or a SNAKE in SNOWFLAKE.

You know there is NOISE in TELEVISION
and AIR in RADIO ...

But imagine finding TOES in CLOSET

or a SOW in SHOWER

or a GARTER in REFRIGERATOR!

You might even find PEAR in CARPET

or FRUIT in FURNITURE.

And speaking of fruit...

Here are some of the things you can find
in different fruit.

There's a CAP in PEACH

and a GEAR in ORANGE.

A LEMON in WATERMELON

and MOLE in LEMON.

CART in APRICOT

and APE in PEAR.

Here's something interesting:

You can find a PAL

          in APPLE

You can find HER

          in CHERRY...

But to find HIM

          see the next page.

In the animal world

you can find HIM in CHIMPANZEE.
In TIGER you can find TIE.
In ELEPHANT you can find PLANE.
In HIPPOPOTAMUS there is SPOUT.
In CAMEL there is LACE.
And in WHALE there is LAW!

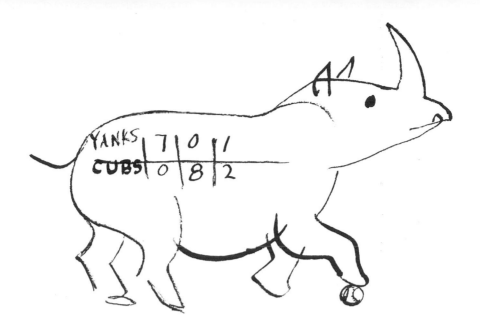

By this time you will not be surprised
to find

OIL in LION
DOOR in CROCODILE
MONEY in MONKEY
WASP in SPARROW
NOOK in KANGAROO
FIRE in GIRAFFE
MAP in PUMA
LOAF in BUFFALO
SCORE in RHINOCEROS.
But although you can find WOLF in FLOWER
that's really for the next page...

In the world of flowers

did you know there was LOVE in VIOLET?

Or PIE in PETUNIA?

Or for that matter a ROSE in HORSE?

There is IDEA
in DANDELION

PONY in PEONY

HAIL in DAHLIA

GIRL in MARIGOLD

DANGER in GARDENIA.

And in CHRYSANTHEMUM
as you can well imagine
you can find MUCH!

Another interesting place to look
for words is in the months.

For instance . . .
In JANUARY you can naturally find YARN.
In FEBRUARY you can find FUR.

You might find RAM in MARCH
And you're likely to find PAIL
in APRIL

Imagine finding MA in MAY
or the UN in JUNE.

In JULY you can't find anything! But
since JULY is named after JULIUS CAESAR
we can look inside of JULIUS ...
and find SULU (a Filipino native).

There's GAS in AUGUST

and PETS in SEPTEMBER

OCTOBER has BOOT

and NOVEMBER has MOVER.

And good old DECEMBER has DEER.

We can also find some interesting words
in the days of the week.

In SUNDAY
you can find SAND

in MONDAY you can find MANY

and in TUESDAY
it's easy to find DUST.

WEDNESDAY
has SEDAN

there is TRAY
    in THURSDAY

and FAIRY
in FRIDAY.

SATURDAY
has STAR.

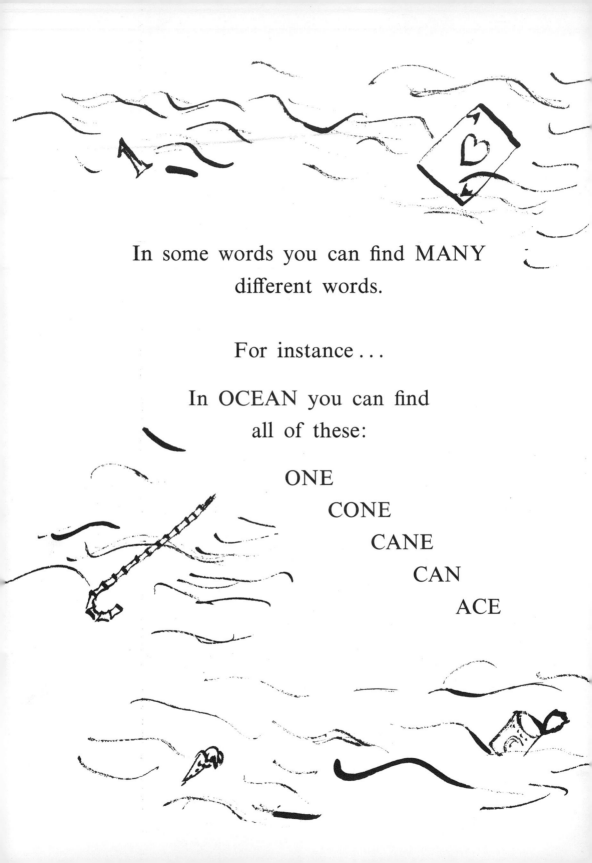

In some words you can find MANY
different words.

For instance...

In OCEAN you can find
all of these:

ONE

CONE

CANE

CAN

ACE

And in EARTH there is

HARE
EAR
HEART
RAT
HEAT
HART
TEAR
HAT

All over the world there
are words to find.

Let's examine some countries...

In FRANCE there is CAFE.
and in ARGENTINA there is GIANT
BELGIUM has GUM
and in IRELAND you find NAIL.
In WALES you will find SEA
and in ENGLAND there is GALE.
HOLLAND has DOLL
and CHILE has ICE.
CHINA has INCH
and
MEXICO
has
MICE.

You can find COLT in SCOTLAND
MARE in DENMARK
and PURR in PUERTO RICO.

There's LARIAT in AUSTRALIA
and WAND in NEW ZEALAND.

In CANADA you'll find AND
and in LAOS, ALSO.

How about trying to find out
what is in your name?
Or in your friend's name?

You might find some of these...
There's SAIL in MELISSA
and OGRE in ROGER.

There is FERN
in JENNIFER
CLAM in MICHAEL
and COAL in CAROL.

There's DARN in ARNOLD
HORSE in CHRISTOPHER
TOY in TIMOTHY
DIN in DENNIS
and KEY in KERRY.

And you can find . . .
YES in SHELLEY, NO in JOHN
and MAYBE in MAYBELLE

A GOOD WAY TO START A GAME WITH
YOUR FRIENDS WOULD BE TO PICK
OUT A LONG WORD AND SEE
WHO CAN FIND THE MOST
HIDDEN WORDS

For instance, what's inside of . . .

ARITHMETIC

or

DICTIONARY

or

ENCYCLOPEDIA?

OF COURSE
YOU COULD STOP AT ANY PAGE IN
THIS BOOK AND USE IT TO START A GAME.

Now here's something that may
surprise you . . .

Look what you find inside of

'inside'

?

END!